National and World Celebrations

Ian Rohr

A+

Smart Apple Media
P.O. Box 3263
Mankato, MN, 56002

First published in 2010 by
MACMILLAN EDUCATION AUSTRALIA PTY LTD
15–19 Claremont St, South Yarra, Australia 3141

Visit our web site at www.macmillan.com.au or go directly to www.macmillanlibrary.com.au

Associated companies and representatives throughout the world.

Copyright © Ian Rohr 2010

Library of Congress Cataloging-in-Publication Data

Rohr, Ian.
    National and global celebrations / Ian Rohr.
        p. cm. -- (Celebrations around the world)
    Includes index.
    ISBN 978-1-59920-538-0 (library binding)
    1. Festivals--Cross-cultural studies--Juvenile literature. I. Title.
    GT3933.R634 2011
    394.26--dc22
                                2009042143

Publisher: Carmel Heron
Managing Editor: Vanessa Lanaway
Editor: Michaela Forster
Proofreader: Kirstie Innes-Will
Designer: Kerri Wilson (cover and text)
Page layout: Pier Vido
Photo researcher: Wendy Duncan
Production Controller: Vanessa Johnson

Manufactured in China by Macmillan Production (Asia) Ltd.
Kwun Tong, Kowloon, Hong Kong
Supplier Code: CP January 2010

Acknowledgments
The author and the publisher are grateful to the following for permission to reproduce copyright material:

Cover photograph: Children waving flags for an Independence Day ceremony in the Gaza Strip, © Shaul Schwarz/Getty Images

AAP Image/The Wilderness Society, 29; ACT Heritage Library, 19; © Corbis, 23; © /Lindsey Parnaby/Corbis, 20; © Ariel Skelley/Corbis, 11; © Joseph Sohm/Visions of America/ Corbis, 14; Fairfaxphotos/Andrew De La Rue, 28; © Eitan Abramovich/AFP/Getty Images, 15; © Stephen Chernin/Getty Images, 22; © Vladimir Rys/ Bongarts/Getty Images, 25; © Shaul Schwarz/Getty Images, 1, 6; © Prakash Singh/AFP/Getty Images, 13; © Cameron Spencer/Getty Images Sport, 24; © Stockbyte/Getty Images, 4; © Bob Thomas/Getty Images, 26; © Jupiter Unlimited/Photos.com, 5; Newspix, 7; Newspix/ Robert Pozo, 8; Newspix/Lyndon Mechielsen, 9; Newspix/Stuart McEvoy, 16; Newspix/David Geraghty, 17; photolibrary/ Alain Evrard, 12; photolibrary/Alamy/Steve Allen Travel Photography, 18; © Shutterstock, 10; © Shutterstock/Elena Elisseeva, 21; © Shutterstock/Jonathan Larsen, 27; © Shutterstock/Kevin Renes, 30.

While every care has been taken to trace and acknowledge copyright, the publisher tenders their apologies for any accidental infringement where copyright has proved untraceable. Where the attempt has been unsuccessful, the publisher welcomes information that would redress the situation.

6091

Contents

When a word is printed in **bold**, you can look up its meaning in the Glossary on page 31.

Celebrations

Celebrations are events that are held on special occasions. Some are events from the past that are still celebrated. Others celebrate important times in our lives or activities, such as music.

Birthdays are special events that many people celebrate.

Some celebrations involve only a few people.
Others involve whole cities or countries.
Large celebrations take place across the world.

New Year's Eve is celebrated all around
the world with fireworks.

What Are National and World Celebrations?

National celebrations are events where a whole country takes part. A world celebration is an event that takes place across the world.

Many countries, such as Israel, celebrate the day they were discovered or became independent.

Many national celebrations remember special events in a country's history. World celebrations can be held for religious reasons, or to celebrate a **culture** or sport.

Many religions have big world celebrations, such as Catholic World Youth Day.

Australia Day, Australia

Australia Day is a national celebration of when Europeans first came to Australia to live. It takes place every year on January 26. This was when the **First Fleet** arrived in Australia in 1788.

Some Australians celebrate their country and culture on Australia Day.

Many **indigenous** Australians do not celebrate Australia Day. This is because they believe it was the day their land was **invaded**. Some people call this day Invasion Day.

Many indigenous Australians hold separate events on January 26.

Fourth of July, United States

The Fourth of July is an American national celebration. It celebrates the day the **Declaration of Independence** was approved in 1776. It is also called **Independence** Day.

The Fourth of July celebrates the signing of the Declaration of Independence many years ago.

The Fourth of July is a holiday, and schools and shops are closed. Many Americans celebrate their history and culture with their families and friends.

Children take part in Fourth of July parades in many American towns and cities.

Independence Day, India

India celebrates its independence from Britain on August 15 every year. The Prime Minister gives a speech to the Indian people. There are also flag-raising **ceremonies** and parades.

Large crowds watch the parades on Indian Independence Day.

Schools are open on Independence Day. Students take part in ceremonies and learn about India's independence. They also sing the Indian national anthem.

School students wave the Indian flag on Independence Day.

Columbus Day, the Americas

Columbus Day is celebrated every October in the **Americas**. People remember the day that the Spanish explorer Christopher Columbus first arrived in the Americas. Some towns celebrate with parades.

CRISTOFORO COLOMBO

A statue of Christopher Columbus, who arrived in the Americas in 1492.

Many indigenous people of the Americas do not celebrate Columbus Day. This is because they believe their people were treated unfairly after Columbus arrived.

Some indigenous people of the Americas hold separate events on Columbus Day.

Anzac Day, Australia and New Zealand

Anzac Day is held in Australia, New Zealand, and some Pacific islands. It is held each year on April 25. This was when Anzac soldiers landed at Gallipoli, Turkey, in 1915.

On Anzac Day, people go to dawn services to remember those who died in wars.

On Anzac Day, members of the **military** take part in parades. There are also special acts to remember those killed or injured. These include laying **wreaths** at **war memorials**.

Parades are a very important part of Anzac Day.

Guy Fawkes Night, United Kingdom

Guy Fawkes Night is a celebration that began in the United Kingdom. It remembers a man called Guy Fawkes. He tried to blow up the Houses of Parliament on November 5, 1605.

Guy Fawkes Night is celebrated in the United Kingdom with bonfires and fireworks.

Guy Fawkes Night was celebrated with bonfires and fireworks for many years. Today, this is not allowed in most countries, because fireworks can be dangerous.

In many places, people once lit bonfires on Guy Fawkes Night.

Remembrance Day

Remembrance Day is held in many countries on November 11 each year. This was the day World War I ended in 1918. Remembrance Day ceremonies honor people killed in wars.

People are silent for two minutes at 11:00 A.M. on Remembrance Day.

On Remembrance Day, people wear poppies as a sign of remembrance. Poppies grew on the battlefields in Europe during World War I.

On Remembrance Day, poppies are used to show respect for people killed at war.

Kwanzaa

Kwanzaa (say *kwan-za*) is a world celebration of African culture. It is held for one week in December. Kwanzaa is celebrated in countries with large numbers of African people.

African dances are part of Kwanzaa celebrations.

Kwanzaa started in the United States in 1966 but has spread to many other countries. During the week, people have large feasts and give presents.

Seven candles are lit during Kwanzaa week—one for each day of the celebration.

Olympic Games

The Olympic Games is a major worldwide sporting celebration. Countries put aside their differences during the games. It is held every four years, in a different city each time.

Most of the world's nations take part in the Olympic Games.

Thousands of athletes from around the world compete in either summer or winter sports. Large numbers of people come to watch the sports events.

Many tourists travel to the host city to see the Olympic Games.

Football World Cup

The Football World Cup is a big soccer competition.
It is held every four years in a different country.
The Football World Cup usually lasts for one month.

Hundreds of thousands of people watch
Football World Cup matches.

Many players and visitors come from around the world to join in the celebration. Millions of people also watch the Football World Cup on television.

Fans of the winning team cheer loudly at the Football World Cup.

World Environment Day

World Environment Day is held every year on June 5. It teaches people about caring for the environment. An organization called the **United Nations** started the day in 1972.

Tree planting takes place all around the world on World Environment Day.

Each year, the celebrations are held in a different city. People from all over the world attend. There are large meetings and other special activities, such as **rallies** and concerts.

Thousands of people take part in rallies on World Environment Day.

Try This!

Find the answers to these questions in the book.
(You can check your answers on page 32.)

1. Why is American Independence Day held on July 4?
2. When is India's Independence Day?
3. Who is remembered on Anzac Day?
4. How is Guy Fawkes Night celebrated?
5. What does Kwanzaa celebrate?

Try This Activity

Next time you celebrate a special occasion with your friends or family, ask yourself:

- Why are you celebrating?
- How long have people been celebrating this event?
- Are there other places in the world where people celebrate the event?

Glossary

Americas	the region that includes all of North, Central, and South America
ceremonies	activities that take place on special occasions
culture	way of living
Declaration of Independence	the document that said America is to be a free country
First Fleet	the 11 ships that first sailed from Britain to Australia
independence	freedom from the rule of another country
indigenous	the first people to live in a country or region
invaded	attacked by people from another country or area
military	soldiers, or those who fought in wars
rallies	events where large numbers of people come together and demand action
remembrance	the act of remembering
United Nations	an organization that most countries belong to
war memorials	special sites to remember those who have served in wars
wreaths	flowers and leaves arranged in a circle

Index

Answers to the Quiz on Page 3

1 This is the date the Declaration of Independence was signed in 1776.
2 On August 15 each year
3 Those who were killed or injured in wars
4 With bonfires and fireworks
5 African culture